A Glimpse Into My Heart

Mission: To Proclaim Transformation and Truth

Published by: Transformed Publishing
Website: www.transformedpublishing.com
Email: transformedpublishing@gmail.com

Copyright © 2020 by Babette Bailey

All rights reserved solely by the author. No part of this book may be reproduced, stored in a retrieval system, or transmitted in any form or by any means without expressed written permission of the author.

Cover Design by Jeff and Brenda Williams

Scripture is taken from the New King James Version ®. Copyright © 1982 by Thomas Nelson. Used by permission. All rights reserved.

ISBN: 978-1-953241-03-0
Printed in the U.S.A.

A Glimpse Into My Heart

Poems of Inspiration

Babette Bailey

Acknowledgements

I want to acknowledge all my family, friends, associates, and even people I didn't know who have encouraged me, believed in me, invested in me, and inspired me.

I am very thankful for every opportunity I have had to share the poems I have written. I love poetry and enjoy the positive and inspiring feedback I have received when sharing at church gatherings, parties, women's events, and schools.

Thank you to everyone who has helped me, encouraged me, and invested in seeing me reach my goals for this book and those that will follow. Your blessings of comfort and contributions are greatly appreciated. They definitely have, and will continue to, make this book and those that follow a success.

Introduction

Basically, this poetry collection is a result of many different experiences I have had. There is no main focus, other than God and this journey of life, within the writings. I think if we look closely, we can see God in every experience we go through. God is always teaching, encouraging, blessing, molding and shaping, disciplining, comforting, using, helping, and filling us.

I find the many different perspectives people can have looking at the same thing intriguing. We can gain a lot, when we take the time to see things from a different point of view.

For all the poetry lovers: I hope you enjoy my style of writing. For those who have dreams that seem too hard to achieve, I hope that you will be encouraged. Always remember, *with God all things are possible*; give *it* your all.

And for those who think they just stumbled upon this book: maybe it's not by chance, but there is something significant in it for you. God bless you all and thank you for giving me a chance to express a glimpse of my heart.

To God be the Glory,

Babette Bailey

Encouraging Scriptures

*Jesus said to him, "If you can believe, all things
are possible to him who believes."
Mark 9:23*

*Delight yourself also in the LORD,
And He shall give you the desires of your heart.
Psalm 37:4*

*"Ask, and it will be given to you;
seek, and you will find;
knock, and it will be opened to you.
For everyone who asks receives,
and he who seeks finds,
and to him who knocks it will be opened…
how much more will your Father who is in heaven
give good things to those who ask Him!
Matthew 7:7-8, 11*

Table of Contents

Poem	Title
1	What Will You Do With Your Invitation
2	Change
3	Why
4	The Clouds
5	From Me To You
6	Beginnings
7	Discipline (In Love)
8	Inspiration
9	This Building
10	I Know He Can
11	Be Encouraged
12	Try Again
13	Shoulda, Woulda, Coulda
14	You Are
15	Both Are Needed To Make One
16	What Would You Die For
17	I'm Growing
18	Away From You
19	Your Wedding Day
20	Happy Birthday My Little Girl
21	Your Latest Arrival
22	Friends
23	Baby's Christening
24	How
25	Beat
26	It's Been Nice
27	This Christmas
28	Doing Time
29	Because Of You
30	I Confess
31	You're Blessed
32	You're Appreciated
33	What About Him
34	Only You Lord
35	"Never Giving In"
36	Today's Friend

Table of Contents

Title	Poem
When You Overcome	37
The New Kid	38
My Christmas Poem	39
Half	40
One In A Million	41
What Christmas Is To Me	42
Hands Of Love	43
You're Beautiful	44
Bless Me Lord	45
A Tree	46
Dark Times	47
Young vs. Old	48
Don't Doubt	49
Hearing From God	50
Happy Birthday	51
Just Say Yes	52
Something About You	53
To Belong	54
The Best Gift	55
Uniquely You	56
To Comfort You	57
Let It Go	58
With Christ	59
As Your Bride	60
A Woman of Virtue	61
God's Laborers	62
Don't Ever Give Up	63
Who Lord, But You	64
I Pray	65
Before	66
Dark And Light	67
Immature	68
Faces	69
Sisters	70
Darling I Love You	71
Love, Tell Me Where You Are	72

Poem 1 ♡

What Will You Do With Your Invitation

*You're invited
The doors are open
No more waiting
For what you've been hoping
Dare to believe
Dare to step out
Dare to receive
What you've dreamed about
This is your season
God has said yes
And He's waiting for you
You're His special guest
So don't hesitate
Don't procrastinate
Your invitation awaits
So don't be late*

♡ *Poem 2*

Change

Change, are you ready?
You've asked for it to come
And now that it has come to you
You're feeling kind of numb
You want to reevaluate, rethink things, redecide
Don't worry, that's quite normal, just try to enjoy the ride
Yes, it's gonna take some time to get adjusted to
But it will sure be worth it all when you finally do
Just focus on the positive, push aside those negative things
They're only there to keep you from the good life wants to bring
And yes, there's going to be some sacrificing too
Some giving here and there, but it's nothing you can't do
And once you've had a chance to let it all sink in
Remember that you wanted it, so give it all you can
And as always, put your trust in God
He knows what's best for you
He brought you through this far
And there's nothing He can't do
So thank Him and remember that it's because of Him we breathe
It's because of Him we feel, we hope, and can do all things

Babette Bailey

Poem 3

Why

Why do I care? I asked myself
And then I turned to God
He said because you have My loving Spirit in your heart
Well God, why do I feel for them
When it's them who have done wrong?
Because, He said, you understand, for you too were once far gone
Well how can I be upset one moment
And laughing in the next?
Because My child, My Spirit of love forgives and forgets
I guess I'm like a child Lord
Full of whys and concerns
Now I understand why kids ask so many whys they want to learn
I'm glad I am Your child Lord
And Your patience is so vast
Because I have so many whys that I have yet to ask
Why the flowers? Why the rain?
Why the summer? Why the spring?
Is it because You like to decorate and rearrange things?
Why the teachers? Why the doctors?
Why the planes? Why helicopters?
Is it because, like You, we have visions and dreams inside of us?
Why did You make me Lord?
What's Your plan for my destiny?
Are you writing and rewriting
According to my faith and deeds?
Well Lord, I know that You are love
And my life is in Your hands
I thank You for taking the time to listen and help me understand
I thank You for Your Promises
I know they will hold true
I cannot promise You no more whys
But I'll bring them all to You

A Glimpse Into My Heart

The Clouds

The clouds may be the angels' transportation
Racing them every day to their jobs
To work throughout the day and night
Whatever job they're assigned by God
The clouds may be the angels themselves
Keeping watch and protection over all
Rushing urgently in when there's an urgent need
Carrying supplies to meet every call
The clouds may be the breath of God
The words He has breathed in our lives
For some it's the end of life on this earth
While for others it's answers to their cries
Then the clouds may be the tears of God
Welling up as His heart is breaking
As He looks over all the corruption
And cries at all the wrong in His creation
I listen to the clouds, sometimes they whisper
Sometimes they're very upset
They shout with warnings and groan with moanings
But they also give soft and gentle compliments
I wonder what happens when the clouds aren't there
And the sky looks clear and smooth
Are the clouds at rest or at work somewhere else
Or with God somewhere far above the blue
I may never be sure of all the reasons for the clouds
But I know they're from the Heavenly One
And whatever job they're assigned by God
I know will be a job well done

Babette Bailey

Poem 5 ♡

From Me To You

I haven't forgotten where I came from
And what I used to be
And I know you doing the things I used to do
You're not any worse than me
But it's because I know what lies ahead
If you don't change your ways
That I warn you and try to guide you
So you won't pay the prices I've paid
If it seems sometimes I'm too strict or harsh
Let me tell you how bad it could be
Death, disease, prison, even addiction
You have eyes look and see
Do you ever wonder why the hurt and pain,
Disease, crime and death?
Have you wondered enough to seek understanding?
Or do you just act like it's not there?
There are laws of living, and there's no escape
They apply to all who live
If I don't teach you and discipline you
Believe me, someone else will
So please, take these words in love
And try to understand
What I'm saying is the more discipline we have
The less we end up paying

From Me To You

Poem 6

Beginnings

I think of when a baby is born, how fearful he must be
Coming from the warmth and comfort of all he's known and seen
His birth, such an unpleasant thing, although he won't recall
How tight the squeeze, how hard the push through the birthing walls
Then being slapped on his bottom and taken from his mother
Must feel like an experience from which he'll never, ever recover
All the new sights and the new sounds must be overwhelming
These changes though, are good for all, and bring those new beginnings
As this new life grows, think of all he will go through
All his firsts, all the fears of all that will be new
His first steps, afraid to let go of his mother's hand
But soon feeling good because he has learned how to stand
The first time he takes a fall he sits and thinks a bit
Then decides it wasn't so bad and keeps trying till he gets it
His first day at school, though it seems too big a risk
Turns out to be a blast, playing with all the other kids
His first dive in the pool, gasping and reaching for help
Turned out to be worth the dare, cause now he can swim by himself
Riding his bike for the first time, without the training wheels
He knew he had to do it though and how good it's made him feel
His first date, his first kiss, his first dream come true
Very nervous, so unsure but still he made it through
His first fight, his first spanking kind of were the same
Cause they shed new light on things about how not to play life's game
Now he's all grown up, but changes still occur
Yes they're still uncomfortable because they're still his firsts
As he looks back over his life, every fear he's had to face
He'll make a mental note how though fearful he escaped
He came to be, he learned to walk, he took some risks, he took some falls
But through it he was strengthened, through it he realized
That changes though quite fearful helped to make him wise
Now as he goes along, as life's changes have their way
I know he's focusing on the good and positive day by day
And in his mind the achievements that started as fearful firsts
Are now the successes those beginnings caused him to birth

Babette Bailey

Discipline
(In Love)

I cannot condemn him
Because of the wrong I've done
I cannot belittle him
Because of whence I come from
I cannot judge him
Because I too am under the eye
Of the Almighty Judge
In that courtroom in the sky

But God You've given me
This responsibility
How can I do what You ask
Without the authority
What's that You say In love
In obedience and faith
And not to worry, doubt or fear
For You will guide the way
Discipline in love
Do not do evil for evil
Don't give full vent to anger
Let Your command be my will

Thank You for Your instruction
Your discipline, Your amazing grace
I'll do my best, but please Lord
Change me from my way

♡ Poem 8

Inspiration

An angel of God, disguised without knowing
Sent to meet my needs, though mine weren't even showing
Thought it was you who needed comfort and peace
But God was only using you to speak to my needs
For it was I who was distraught and under attack
So God spoke to you and used you to help me get back
Though I didn't realize and neither did you
Till after things were said and done, what we'd went through
We never saw Him coming, we only saw His back
But I knew that He'd been with us, by where I was now at
My frustration had left me, my peace had been restored
I was no longer focused on my problems, nor you on yours
I thank Him for using you, but I want you to know too
When you least expect it, God will be using you
Know that every situation isn't necessarily about you
But a point, a plan, a purpose is the reason you're going through
So stay strong in the Lord, trust Him no matter what
Inspiration of God sent from me to you in love

Babette Bailey

This Building

I watched as He went through my life
Tearing down and rebuilding
He brought things in that helped with
The remodeling and mending
The stripping was hard
Being broken was tough
But now I can see
How it straightened me up
He took away things
That didn't fit in
And reshaped them according to
His deed and plan
He's still not done
For as time goes on
There are still things that need
To be changed and redone
Some things that get old,
Or no longer fit
Some things simply need
Touching up a bit
Some things refreshing
Some things renewed
Some things just dusting
Or polishing will do
He keeps me in order
And all cleaned up
Takes good care of His house
That He has built with His love

♡ *Poem* 10

I Know He Can

With one touch of His hand
I know that He can calm the sea
So patiently I wait for Him
To calm the waves in me
With one wave of His hand
He can make the wind be still
Wish He'd kindly touch my wind
Make it surrender to His will
With just one little whisper
He could change all my darkness to light
He could alter all my days
Change the rest of my life
He could make all my enemies
Turn and flee, run away
He could bring a smile of joy
Or peace and bless my every day
He could move any obstacle
No matter how big or high
He could light up my way
When my way seems dark as night
He could open up the skies
Rain abundantly on me
Things far greater and wonderful
Than I imagined they could be
Yes I know there is nothing
In this world He cannot do
So I wait for Him to speak
To wave His hand and help me through
To lift my heavy burdens
That are much too big for me
To expose and remove everything
That sometimes I can't see

Babette Bailey

Poem 11 ♡

Be Encouraged

I share your loss today
I share your grief and pain
My heart goes out to you
For the loved one that's gone away

But be encouraged today
And always keep this thought
That God is a righteous judge
And He looks into the heart

I'm sure He'd say today
That all though there was some sin
The heart was pure as gold
And well worth taking in

A Glimpse Into My Heart

♡ Poem 12

Try Again

*It's the times we spend alone
The times we have to cry
The times that we endure
The times we're not so high*

*That we learn to appreciate
And learn to be strong
And most of all we learn
How to keep on keeping on*

*Remember trials gone past
Some you won, some you lost
Sometimes you hardly paid
But other times it really cost*

*Though we have to cry sometimes
And sometimes we don't win
There's always hope if we hang in there
And try, try again*

Babette Bailey

Shoulda, Woulda, Coulda

If only I had taken heed
To the words I shoulda
I wouldn't still be thinking of doing
All the things I coulda
It pains me so to think
That only if I woulda
Sacrificed and paid the price
The things that I coulda
I coulda been successful by now
I certainly think I shoulda
Instead of ending up another
Shoulda, woulda, coulda
I've watched other people
Go from all the things they coulda
To broken dreams and failure
Cause they didn't do as they shoulda
I've listened to their stories
They know that if they woulda
Only made the right choices
They wouldn't be crying I coulda
So do what you can to make sure
You don't become one of the oulda's
I've warned you so it's your fault
If you become a shoulda, woulda, coulda

♡ Poem 14

You Are

Lord You are the potter, You make the day
You open doors, You make the way
You are the light, You hold the key
You are the success and the opportunity
You are the mender of all broken hearts
You're the replacement of all broken parts
You're the beginning and You are the end
You are the prayer and the amen
You are the answer, You are the truth
You are the old and You are the new
You are the promises and You are the hope
You are tomorrows and long, long agos
You're the creator, You're summer and spring
You are the Savior, the Prince, and the King
You are the need and the supply
You're the hello and the good-bye
You're the main course, the dessert, the entrée
You're the entertainer, the encore, the ole
You are the bank, You are the teller
You are the merchandise, You are the seller
You are the music, You are the song
You are the everything, that's why I'm holding on

Babette Bailey

Poem 15 ♡

Both Are Needed To Make One

I see the light is good, for we work and we play
But the dark is good too, for we rest from our day
And the two make one, without both as we have seen
A day is just not fulfilled or complete

I see the husband and the wife, their roles so unique
One does this or that, whichever the case may be
But the two make one, and unless they both agree
They'll never be a team, they'll never be complete

The employer, the employee, both serve, both receive
Both giving that they both might fulfill both needs
Still the two come together for both to succeed
And without them both, they're both incomplete

If bad wasn't so, then how could good be
For the purpose of one is so that the other can be seen
And the two compare, two meanings, but one main idea
Both of them are needed, for both to be clear

I think in every situation there's some good and some bad
Some dark and some light some joy and some sad
I see some positive, some negative, some yes and some no
Some real, some unreal, some must stay and some must go

In life we see that we are born and we must die
The dark of it is, in what way and at what time
In life we obtain much success along our way
But the dark of it is the endurance that it takes

We love, we hate, we laugh, we cry
The seasons come and go but they make up our lives
There are winners and losers for every race
But where is the finish line and who sets the pace

Then there are people that come and that go
Some you wish could always stay, some you wish you'd never known
Still all of these things, good or bad, are all a part
Of the rhythm and the beats we need to regulate our hearts

A Glimpse Into My Heart

♡ *Poem 16*

What Would You Die For

*What would you die for?
Is that what life is all about?
Sacrificing for someone or something
No matter who or how*

*I see people dying for love
Some even for their country
Some for our God above
Some for hopes, dreams or money*

*Some for food, some for clothes
Some for evil, some don't know
Some for drugs, some for lying
Some for sex, some for flying*

*Some for their children
Some for their jobs
Some for relief from
Their troubled hearts*

*Some for taking risks
For daring to go beyond
Some for protecting others
Making sure justice is done*

*Some for doing wrong
Some for doing right
Some refusing to lose
Some refusing to fight*

*Some say there are many things
For which they'd give their lives
But until their time has come
They may not have even realized*

Babette Bailey

Poem 17 ♡

I'm Growing

I remember being so fearful at times
So troubled, unhappy, anxious, and wrong
I remember calling on God to help me
I just wanted those feelings to be gone

Time after time He answered my call
Restoring peace to my mind
Even now I don't know if I truly see
How good God is and how kind

I'm sure I've thanked Him, I'm sure I've been grateful
If only those feelings would last
Instead they seem to just slip away
Somewhere deep in my past

Though I really don't want to carry
Those kinds of burdens every day
I know if I thought of them more
I'd be more sincere when I pray

Today was one of those days
God spared me once again
Revealing the love, the power and mercy
He holds within His hands

As I think of what could have happened
How things could have turned out
I know that thank you isn't enough
I should really rejoice and shout

But until I reach that point
Of praising Him as I should
I hope my heartfelt thank you
Will do just as good

I know that I know that I know
He has all power in His hands
So why I worry and doubt
I may never understand

But, I'm growing

A Glimpse Into My Heart

♡ *Poem* 18

Away From You

I went away, thought I could make it on my own
Oh Lord, but today, I need to come home
To be in the comfort of Your arms
For I've been so abused by this world's harm
If only I had listened, took heed to Your words
I could have avoided these heavy burdens
Even when You helped me, I still turned away
I gave in to temptations day after day
Choosing to do wrong though hearing You say
How much must you endure before you turn My way
Still I went on finding every excuse I could
Said I just needed time to change like I should
I told You Lord, I couldn't do it on my own
But the truth is I wanted those things to go on
I went away Lord, thought I could make it on my own
Oh Lord, but today, I need to come home

Babette Bailey

Poem 19 ♡

Your Wedding Day

One of the biggest moments in a woman's life
Has now come to you
One of the dreams you've always dreamed of
Is now coming true

Remember the things you feel today
Are good, but keep in mind
All the things that mama said
The do's, the don'ts, and the why's

May your happiness last
May your heart be cheered
May your love be renewed
With each passing year

Now much congratulations are due
So here's to you and yours
To a life of love, of peace, of joy
On your wedding day and forever more

A Glimpse Into My Heart

♡ *Poem 20*

Happy Birthday My Little Girl

*I still call you my little girl
Though you're not so little, I know*

*You're still my precious little jewel
Though you're not so little, I know*

*You're still my little princess
Though you're not so little, I know*

*You still like mama's little gifts
Though not too little, I know*

*I'm still the one who loves you
You're not too big, you know*

*I'm still the one who cares for you
You're not too big, you know*

*I'm still the one who listens to you
You're not too big, you know*

*I'm still the one who buys for you
Just making sure you know*

Babette Bailey

Your Latest Arrival

Congratulations on your latest arrival!
I know you've got a bundle of joy
Bet you've already forgotten the labor, the pain
You thought that you couldn't endure
As you kiss those little cheeks
I know that you're filled with awe
So congratulations on the miracle you've received
From our miracle working God

♡ Poem 22

Friends

Friends share the goofy times
And each other's bloopers
Friends share the happy times
Those times dearest to us

Friends always share a smile
Even when they're apart
Reflecting on the things
That have really touched their hearts

I thought of you today friend
And all we used to do
Thought I'd share that thought with you
Thought you could use a smile too

Babette Bailey

Baby's Christening

Giving back to the Lord
What He has given you
With this bundle of life's joy
Rededication is due

To the Lord it means you trust Him to guide
And watch this little one through
Life's mazes and life's mysteries
Just as He's trusting you

To you it lets you know
That you're off to the right start
Bringing this child back to the Lord
Means you're striving to do your part

For the child it means a special shield
Is being placed upon their life
To protect and keep them
Until they learn to decide and to do what's right

May God's blessings be with all of you!

♡ *Poem 24*

How

How can you win if you never fight
How can it turn day if it's never night
How can you grow up if you're never young
How can you know how to sing if you've never sung
How can you run if you've never walked
How can you be heard if you've never talked
How can you see if you never look
How can you read without a book
How can you stop if you've never started
How can you reunite if you're never parted
How can you grow without a seed
How can you grow without food to eat

Babette Bailey

Poem 25

Beat

*Sometimes the beat is gonna change
It's gonna slow down for a while
Sometimes the beat won't be the same
But remember it's all in God's time
Marching to the beat of the Lord*

*Sometimes the beat feels so good
It's just the kind of pace that you like
But don't get too relaxed remember
We've got to keep up with God's time
Marching to the beat of the Lord*

*We've been running for such a long time
But there are those with brand new lives
They can't keep up if we keep our own pace
So we've got to adjust with God's time
Marching to the beat of the Lord*

Poem 26

It's Been Nice

It's been nice having you for my friend
Just wanted you to know
Your calls and your encouragement
The extra miles you go
Taking time out of your day
To pray that I'll be blessed
But let me tell you what I really
Like about you best

You like me as I am
You're my sister in the Lord
We can talk about anything
Some say that's what friends are for
You're thoughtful and considerate
You're funny and you're sweet
You're a good-hearted friend,
And a lot more, from what I see

I know I've told you thanks
But I felt a special need
To really emphasize how much
Your friendship means to me

Babette Bailey

Poem 27 ♡

This Christmas

This Christmas all I want is
You know what and why
It's the only thing that I don't have
And I sure could use one ni
Ni you know me, nuttin too fancy
Just make sure he's a good fit
Cause I don't wanna have to come back to you
Talking bout trading him in
Ni every year you treat me right
So I can't complain
In fact I can hardly wait to see
This Christmas what you'll bring
I guess I shouldn't ponder tho
On the thought of that thing too long
I'll be done dreamt up something child!
Anyway, let me move on

Ni bless the kids, mom and dad
Yea June Bug and all nem too
Bless the neighbors, bless the poor
You know, like you always do
Not to make it sound selfish
But this year is a special plea
Mama need a special gift
Something just for me
I trust you ni so hook me up
And I know you got good taste
So I'm expecting something sho nuff nice
To be comin round my way

Ni bout that being naughty stuff
And you seeing everything we do
No need in me trying to lie
So can you overlook a thing or two
Cause you know and I know I've made some mistakes
But if you're feeling extra jolly
My stocking will be that tall one that says
All my thanks! Love, Mommy

A Glimpse Into My Heart

♡ Poem 28

Doing Time

Waiting to be released from behind these prison walls
To be free, be with the one I love, and arise from my fall

This heart of mine, this healing process; why does it take so long?
The time I'm doing waiting for my heart to once again be strong

Growing up, one day I know I won't hear that I'm too young
One day it's going to be my way, these feet can't wait to run

My loved one's not doing too good, I pray God send a miracle
Meanwhile I'm doing time hoping and waiting in the walls of this hospital

Where's my spouse Lord? Oh how long it seems I've waited
There seems to be no hope in sight; don't know the last time that I dated

We've been unhappy for so long; it seems like forever
How do we learn to hope again? Be happy Lord, will we ever?

Everybody's doing time, feeling the chains of despair
But don't let go, hold on to God for He really does care

Waiting, praying, hoping, longing, whatever the case may be
Doing time, whoever and whatever is never ever easy

But remember what's good about doing time, is when the times are right
Try to keep that thought in mind when those times are not in sight

Babette Bailey

Because Of You

Roses are red
Violets are blue
My flowers are alive
Because of You

They were wounded so badly
Fading from the rain
But You shined Your light
Of love on them again

I don't know why
You chose to care
But it sure feels good
Having You here

Yeah my roses are red
And my violets are blue
And Jesus I owe
All thanks to You

♡ *Poem* 30

I Confess

Lord I asked You to use me
To share in spreading Your love
But when times got real tough
I wanted to pass the cup

I even said Lord I'm Yours
I submit myself to You
I said Lord speak to me
I'll do what You want me to

I told You mold and shape me
Into something that You could use
But I questioned what You were doing in me
When my life was being made new

I said that I'd keep Your commands
And love You with all my heart
But I failed to meet Your demands
Every time I fell apart

I failed to take You at Your Word
I failed to walk by faith
I failed to trust You in my heart
I failed to hold on and wait

I asked You Lord why this road
Why this thing, why this test
I asked You why so silent Lord
I was wrong now, I confess

Whatever Your will for my suffering
I pray just help me stand
Whatever You'd have me sacrifice
I'll keep trying until I can

Babette Bailey

Poem 31 ♡

You're Blessed

I wonder how you've become so blessed
Your heart so full of love
You must be a close descendant of
The One up above
And like Him I guess you've also got
Some pretty awesome traits
Giving, loving, sacrificial,
Unselfish and helpful ways
You've blessed me time and time again
Never have you said no
You've always been right there for me
You've always helped me grow
I'm moved today with thoughts of how
You give and bless and love
To all you know who have special needs
And to others simply because
I want to be like you someday
I think what you have is priceless
A heart of rare and precious gems
That loves making sacrifices
Thank you for giving in so many ways
You've truly blessed my life
I love you because of all your love
And because you're wonderful and nice
I know I speak for many who
You've blessed with your giving love
When I say I know, you're an angel
God has sent us from above
I thank Him and I thank you
For taking time to care
And for all the times you don't even know
That you were always there

A Glimpse Into My Heart

♡ Poem 32

You're Appreciated

Your light does shine so brightly
When you give so freely of yourself
I see you in so many places
Giving something more precious than wealth
Your love, your time, your treasures
God placed deep down in your soul
To be blessed and used by God
Is more precious than diamonds and gold.
Who can look and not see
That Spirit of God on your life
Who can listen and not hear
His voice coming from deep inside
It's not mine to lift you up
For you're not the Lord I know
But it's such a blessing you're giving
And I wanted to tell you so
And I know that if I've seen it
That somebody else has too
And I know it's ok to encourage someone
Who gives as much as you
So I want you to know your giving
Encourages me so very much
To give, to love, to help
For someone always needs a touch

Babette Bailey

Poem 33

What About Him

*He's quite different he realizes
But he doesn't really understand yet
Why his mind, his feelings, his emotions
Are so different from everyone else
Did he choose to be the way he is
Did he choose to be so odd
He wonders silently to himself
But the answers seem way too hard
Is there anyone that would love him
Or accept him the way he is
Seems only those who are like him
Would even consider being his friends
Longing for love and acceptance
Unable to change though he tries
Soon he gives in to that thing
That he has fought so long to hide
In his heart he hates who he is
But something won't let him die
He knows he can't live in this "perfect" world
So an imperfect one he tries
Is there any hope, he wonders
When he's not even given a chance
Does he even stand a chance
If this is destiny's hand
All he wants is freedom
In his heart, his soul and his mind
But chances are he'll never find it
Unless the love of God is shined
His light of hope, His light of truth
His light of deliverance
His light of love to all the world
I ask you what about him*

A Glimpse Into My Heart

♡ *Poem 34*

Only You Lord

Lord I want to hear from You and only You
Please tell me what You would have me do
Should I go this way or the other
Should I turn back or go further
One says this way, one says that
One says action, another relax
I want to hear from You for myself
I know that You know me and just what's best
Lord I want to hear from You and only You

Babette Bailey

"Never Giving In"
(In Memory of Our Black Historians)

The stripes upon your back
Your sore and aching feet
The scars around your neck
Your pain and suffering
Your stand for righteousness
Your voice to overcome
Your vision for the best
Your battles for freedom
The tears that were shed
The lives that were lost
The things that went unsaid
The miles you had to cross
Your torn and ragged clothing
Your prayers and your pleas
Your sacrifice, your laboring
Your fears, your injuries
The success that was gained
The mountains that were moved
The breaking off of chains
The lives that were renewed
Your dark and lonely nights
Your endurance till the end
Your frustrations and your fights
Thanks for never giving in

♡ Poem 36

Today's Friend

Today I made a friend
She opened up to me
She really fit the description
Of what I think a friend should be
She talked as though she knew me
As if we were good friends
And treated me like family
Even like one of her cousins
I wanted to let her know
She really made my day
To have someone believe in me
Or reach out to me that way
The issue may seem small to you
But to me it says a lot
Cause friends like the one I found today
Are something I haven't got
Me, I'm kind of reluctant
When it comes to making friends
And it takes a special person
For me to treat like kin
And of course I have some friends
Though we don't always get to hang out
Sometimes the things they want to do
Are not the things I'm about
Over the years I've made some friends
And we've gone our separate ways
But Today's Friend is the kind
I know will stay with me always

Babette Bailey

When You Overcome

Once you are strengthened
Strengthen your brother
Once you are comforted
Comfort another
Once you can see
Pray for the blind
Once you believe
Help others find
Once you are healed
Visit the sick
Once you are chosen
Help others get picked

When you overcome
When you reach success
When you are victorious
No! You can't rest
Remember God's purpose
Remember God's plans
Remember God's instructions
And His commands
To love, trust, and always pray
To believe and in all things give thanks
To serve God and share the Good News
Why our Savior was beaten and bruised
Because of a love so strong
A love so great
To give hope for the world
God's Amazing Grace

♡ Poem 38

The New Kid

Don't look at me like that
I won't take none of your mess
I'm not like all the others
So look at your own self
You say I don't act right
And you think that I should change
I think the same about you
You're the one that's strange
What you call behavior
Is how I've learned to survive
If you were in my shoes
You wouldn't even be alive
You live in the suburbs
You have a nice home
Would you still be the same
If dope was all you've known
I don't want you messing with me
So I hope you hear what I say
If you put your hands on me
I hope you don't plan to play
I didn't ask to be here
So if you really want to help
Stop judging and just show me
How to get out of this hell

Ok, I admit
That this is where I was
But now I'm feeling differently
And the reasons are because
I'm learning having control
Is a better way to be
I'm learning to accept you
As you learn to accept me
Being away from home
Was hard on me at first

But I realize what it's done for me
Made me better not worse
I've done lots of time outs
My point card has been addressed
Yes, I'm doing much better
I don't get as depressed
Still sometimes I'm angry
Cause I'm still thinking, "why me"
Would I have turned out better
If my parents cared for me
Still I've learned that lashing out
Isn't the way to go
I have learned self-control
And soon I'm going home
It sounds kind of scary
Cause the block is still the same
But I'm not planning to go back
To doing the same things

Hey look there's a new kid
He reminds me of me
I know he'll be just fine
I know that he will see
The staff here is great
And they really care
And that discipline is the key
To a life we can share
I'd like to tell him just listen
And he'll do very well
That's what someone told me
And it really, really helped
Still I know he's got to go through
And learn the points and the prones
Then before you know it
He too will be going home

Babette Bailey

Poem 39 ♡

My Christmas Poem

*I know this Cat who's jolly and fat
He's got a list, some helpers, and some goods for the askin'
Lots of goods, enough for the world
'Bout this time of year I'm being a real good girl
Some say they believe, while others they don't
So I told this Cat, look, I'll take what they won't
I told him that there's a few other things too
That if he wasn't too busy, I sure could use
Just the thought and the excitement of waking up Christmas Day
And finding that big gift which has my name
Has me running around and wanting to shout
People looking at me like what's she so happy about
I just bless 'em, say honey season's greetings
Christ has been born and 'tis His season!
My kids look at me talking 'bout you ain't no chile'
I say chile' please, don't get me started ni
If I ain't no child, then you ain't neither
I know I'm a big girl, but I'm still a believer
Then they told me, Christmas ain't for you
I told 'em Christ is for all, and His gifts are too
I told 'em I don't care what nobody say
That this is between me and the Big Guy anyway
Then I went on talking and mumbling to myself
Before I knew it, I yelled, not even the Grinch himself!
My kids looked at me, and I looked at them back
Then all of us couldn't help but bust out and laugh
But they knew that I had meant what I said
It wasn't just something coming from my head
I felt and believed that thing in my soul
And I don't care if the whole world knows
I believe in Christ and His gifts too
And every year I'm reminded by this seasonal tribute
Even non-believers that see the displays
Feel the love and the excitement that's spread in Jesus' name
Well, I've got to go, got to finish my tree
Ni, remember it's all a matter of what you believe*

Merry Christmas

A Glimpse Into My Heart

Half

On the outside I'm pretty, something to see
My hair is fixed nice, my clothes are neat
I smile and talk with charm and grace
My skin is smooth on my hands and face

But inside there are scars and battle bruises
There are fears and insecurities too
There are flashbacks of wars and pain from the past
From careless and hurtful loves that didn't last

It has made me strong, yet made me weak
Opened my eyes, yet blinded me
It has made me tough, yet tender too
I'm wiser now, but I'm still going through

So I smile when I see you, cry when I'm alone
I still hope and dream, but still I long
I wanna rush, but I wanna wait
I wanna be brave, but still sometimes I'm afraid

So I brace myself, yet try to prepare
To tell you the truth, I'm ready, but scared
I guess it depends on what you see
Is my glass half full or half empty

Babette Bailey

One In A Million

Some may have thought that you were just another seed
Dropped in the soil to grow
Though you seemed to sprout much like every other seed
There was much more inside that didn't show
All you've grown through, a lot I know
All the dirt and the storms of life
But maybe it took all you've endured
For you to rise so high
Who could have known you were that one in a million
That one that would rise above the rest
Who could have known that despite how things looked
You would one day be "Success"
And who would have thought you'd be that one in a million
That one that would feed so many lives
Who would have thought that God would choose you
The one that seemed least in so many eyes
I understand that there's something inside
That keeps you soaring high
It's that one in a million spirit
God gives to every one-millionth life

♡ *Poem 42*

What Christmas Is To Me

*Well,
There was a time when Christmas to me
Was a time to just receive
Then as I grew, I thought of Christmas
As a time for special things
At times I've felt that Christmas was
A time for little kids
From there I went to thinking it was
A time all learned to give
Of course, I've learned now that it's a time
To remember our Savior's birth
And how much that Baby born to us
Is really, really worth
It's indeed a time to celebrate
And a time to rejoice
A time to go and tell the world
To lift up every voice
A time for our lights to shine
A time for all to see
The love, the gifts, the warmth
The cheer we have when we believe
I know it seems such a big fuss
But it's not when you consider
What the whole occasion is for
Christ Jesus, our Lord and Savior
We celebrate our birthdays
Marriages and more
Why not celebrate this time
When Jesus Christ was born
Just a thought, don't go too deep
The choice is up to you
But remember as you give
It will be given unto you*

Babette Bailey

Poem 43 ♡

Hands Of Love

I remember when I didn't give much thought to You at all
Just doing my little thing, thought I was really having a ball
And it's not like I'm doing so much even still today
But I know that You have brought me from a mighty long way
The way I used to talk, I wouldn't want anyone to know
But You washed away that filth and put some new words in my soul
The things I used to do, so degrading and so low
But You caught me as I was falling, held me, and didn't let go
My thoughts were all so evil, full of hate, envy and strife
Full of jealousy and perversion too, deceitfulness and lies
But today, Lord I give thanks and praises to You Oh Most High
Though my journey continues on, You have really blessed my life
I feel clean inside and out, addiction free from my old ways
I know Your Spirit is upon me, and that gives me hope for even brighter days
Clean me up Lord, though it hurts being chastened and rebuked
For if You don't I'll destroy myself with the wrong that I do
Thank You Lord for Your grace, thank You Lord for so much
Thank You for watching, guiding and shaping me with Your gentle Hands Of Love

A Glimpse Into My Heart

♡ *Poem 44*

You're Beautiful

You're beautiful asleep
You're beautiful awake
You're beautiful every night
You're beautiful every day

You're beautiful when you smile
You're beautiful when you cry
You're beautiful when you're bold
You're beautiful when you're shy

You're beautiful when you work
You're beautiful when you play
You're beautiful when you're worried
You're beautiful when you're brave

Your beauty is never-ending
Your beauty always shines
Your beauty will never ever cease
At least not in my eyes

Babette Bailey

Poem 45 ♡

Bless Me Lord

Bless me in the morning Lord
Wake me with Your kiss
Early Lord awaken me
Let me hear from Your lips
Nudge me with Your Spirit Lord
Let me feel Your touch
Wake me to spend time with You Lord
Feel the presence of Your love
Talk with me, share Your heart
Whisper in my ear
Tell me again and again
How much You want me near
Hold me in the strength of Your arms
I'm Yours and You are mine
Oh precious Lord You really are
So amazing in my life
Prepare me for the day's journey
Let me start it with You
Thank You in advance Lord
For all You're going to do

A Glimpse Into My Heart

♡ Poem 46

A Tree

Picture yourself as a tree
Wide to the trunk with many branches
Your leaves nice and green
And your height, many inches
You've been standing through the rain
Standing through the storms
Standing through the heat of the sun
Standing is your norm
You've seen many chopped down
Many come and go
Been threatened yourself a time or two
But yet, still you grow
You've had branches that didn't make it
Twigs that fell away
All a part of you but still
Short lived would be their fate
I can't imagine how the rain feels
Beating down with its power
But I know you've come to appreciate
Those refreshing, life-giving showers
You also have a good view
Seen more than your share, I bet
Over-heard a lot I'm sure
Shared a lot of secrets
I bet that it's a good feeling
Being able to give lots of shade
And others looking up to you
Marveling at how you're made
Each branch I imagine as your offspring
Each twig a fresh new life
Each leaf to represent your love
Each looking to you for supply
One day I know you'll be gone
For in time everything fades
I know that you'll be greatly missed
But until that special day
Thank you for enduring
The bugs, the dogs and the unknown
Thank you for what you give and have given
Standing silently strong

Babette Bailey

Poem 47 ♡

Dark Times

How dark the times of heartache can be
You wait for the light you may never see
You cry, you yearn, you search, you pray
But still the darkness won't go away
Why do the dark times come, we wonder
As we curse and despise them, we ponder
But the fact is that dark times will always persist
From day one they were here and still they exist
Dark times come to make the brightness shine
So rest while it's dark, it will leave in due time

♡ *Poem 48*

Young vs. Old

*Most say that being young means being immature
And being old is wisdom for sure
But the older I get, the more that I think
That young vs. old isn't always as it seems
Depending on the circumstances and the topic at hand
Determines who's the wiser, the young or old man
Some young men have seen things, the old may never see
Gone places and experienced things, the old didn't know could be
But I think the advantage that the older man has
Is together his experiences far outweigh and outlast*

Babette Bailey

Don't Doubt

Doubt, the contraction for do-without
What you're saying to yourself is no, not now
You're telling yourself that trying doesn't count
You're saying I probably can't anyhow
If you never try, you will never know
If you think you can't then that's what will show
Believing comes before success
Trying comes before winning and yes
If you've tried, was there any doubt
And if there was don't just do without
Try again and again till you know
There is no doubt, and faith is what shows
Faith, the contraction for favor-with
You're saying that I know this time I'm gonna win

♡ *Poem 50*

Hearing From God

If we whisper to God, will He whisper too
If our hearts repent, what will God's do
If we are angry with Him, will He demand respect
If we humble ourselves, will He show mercy instead

How I long to hear God speak
To know what He wants and thinks of me
To know if I'm doing any of this right
Or if He is pleased just knowing I've tried

Have I ignored the Lord, looking for my yes
When it's not His answer to my request
Have I closed my ears and turned my own way
Because I didn't hear what I wanted Him to say

I guess the truth is I'm not looking for a no
And You're silent cause You don't want to hurt me so
I'll just go back to work and wait till it's time
Then I'll hear Your yes clearly and see all Your signs

Babette Bailey

Poem 51 ♡

Happy Birthday

Every day is your birthday, though today you get a special dessert
Hope this extra that I'm giving makes you happier
You know that you have me, a rare gift I'm giving you each day
But this extra that I'm giving, is to especially celebrate
This day of God's creation, this day He set aside
This day He let the world know that you were on His mind
This day that He reminds you, as well as others too
That He has some very special things, He's giving to only you

A Glimpse Into My Heart

♡ *Poem 52*

Just Say Yes

Let God operate
He's got to make you better
He's got to get on the inside
Cut through your tough outer layer
If you're going to live
You've got to submit and go through
And you can't afford to wait too late
You must decide and move soon
Choosing this operation
Simply requires a yes
Put yourself totally at His mercy
And He will do the rest

Babette Bailey

Something About You

You're like a rose to me
Soft but powerful in charm
Like the thorns of a rose
You protect me with the strength of your arms

Like its colors so deep
Is your love within my heart
Like its smell so sweet
A sweet aroma you are

Like the uniqueness that it holds
You hold your own too
There's something about a rose
And there's something about you

♡ Poem 54

To Belong

To belong, to fit in, to be part of, needed and loved
To belong, to be included, to be invited, to be wanted
What do you do when you don't belong
When where you are, doesn't feel like home
What a feeling of despair
We all need to feel that someone cares
The touch of a hand, the warmth of a smile
Comfort of friends, words that are kind
Come into the House of God
It's an excellent place to start
Invite the Lord into your life
And He'll fill your empty heart

Babette Bailey

Poem 55 ♡

The Best Gift

The best gift that you can give someone
Is the gift of God
Giving God means giving love
That's deep within your heart
Love, that sacrificing, patient,
Caring and forgiving kindness
That will never ever leave you
Even when your life's a mess
Although sometimes love will chasten you
In time you'll see the truth
That nothing else can measure up
To the gift of God's love for you

♡ *Poem 56*

Uniquely You

*Did you know that what makes you uniquely you
Is that purpose that path that only you'll go through
The things that only you will achieve
Your strengths and your possibilities
The lives He'll use only you to touch
Though you may not think that you're enough
But God knew you before you were formed
He purposed you in His mind
Even your name and your days
All your travels and ventures through life
Your smile, your laugh, your tenderness
Your form, your emotions, your charm
Your wit, your trials, your success
Your potential, your faith, your warmth
You're one of God's greatest creations
You're special and uniquely made
And they'll never be another you
Along life's narrow way*

Babette Bailey

To Comfort You

I feel your pain
I know what it's like to long and not understand
To search yourself
And be filled with all kinds of questions with no real answers
But I pray that God will give you that peace
That surpasses all understanding
To fill the void of the one you've lost
To life's unpredictable ending
I know there's no one who can ease the pain
That you're still going through
But I pray that God will give you the needed
Strength and comfort to help you through

Let It Go

You hold that thing too tight
You'll smoother it, let it go

You hold that thing too long
You'll wear it out, let it go

You hold it the wrong way
You'll damage it, let it go

You keep it from being free
It'll escape, so let it go

You try to hide it away
That won't work either, let it go

You never let it breathe
You'll kill it, let it go

Everything has purpose and destiny to fulfill
So know when to let things go and let them be as they will

Babette Bailey

Poem 59 ♡

With Christ

With Christ I can do anything
With Christ I can be free
With Christ I can move mountains
I can go as far as my dreams can dream

With Christ I can change my ways
With Christ I can see better days
With Christ I can overcome pain
As He leads me to His healing embrace

With Christ I am loosed from all
The things that have held me down
With Christ I am made tall
He won't let my heart stay bound

With Christ I am made whole
As He takes me to His breast
He paid the price for my soul
In Him there's peace and rest

In Christ I find joy and love
And good is all I think of
In Christ I can go above
With His special, loving touch

Poem 60

As Your Bride

Lord You chose me to be Your bride
You said You'd have me and never leave my side
And I'm really glad that You love me so much
That's why I've come to accept Your love
You said nothing could take Your love from me
You said You'd be strong when I am weak
You said better or worse, good times or bad
You'd cherish me, and that's why I'm glad
Lord Your love, I don't take lightly
Thank You for giving so generously
As Your bride, I'm submitted to You
To love and obey, to serve and be true

I do, Lord, I commit to You
I do, Lord, receive Your love too
I'll do my best to always do right
And honor this marriage all my life

Babette Bailey

Poem 61 ♡

A Woman of Virtue

A woman of virtue
A woman of class
A woman of God
A woman unmasked
A woman of character
A woman of truth
A woman of example
A woman that's loosed
A woman of vision
A woman of faith
A woman of promise
A woman of praise
A woman of laughter
A woman of touch
A woman of wisdom
A woman of love
A woman of purpose
A woman of strength
A woman of kindness
A woman of confidence
A woman of beauty
A woman of grace
A woman of prayer
A woman of thanks
A wife, A teacher
A daughter, A preacher
A friend, A counselor
A leader, A warrior
We celebrate you woman of virtue
So much that you've become
So many beautiful, wonderful and loving
Blessings all in one

God's Laborers

<u>G</u>ivers of the heart, <u>G</u>ladly they serve
<u>O</u>ptimistic believers, <u>O</u>n fire for God's Word
<u>D</u>elivered and set apart, <u>D</u>etermined they trod
<u>S</u>erving God's calling, <u>S</u>eeking God's heart

<u>L</u>aboring for the needy, <u>L</u>oving everyone
<u>A</u>ppreciating God, and <u>A</u>ll He's done
<u>B</u>oasting for righteousness, <u>B</u>ending the world's ear
<u>O</u>pportunities to help all, <u>O</u>vercome fear
<u>R</u>ewards await them, they're <u>R</u>eady to receive
<u>E</u>ver sharing happiness, <u>E</u>ver setting free
<u>R</u>ejoicing and singing, <u>R</u>eclaiming God's land
<u>S</u>aving all the word, <u>S</u>erving till the end

Babette Bailey

Poem 63 ♡

Don't Ever Give Up

*I know it gets hard and frustrating too
But just keep hanging in there, whatever you do
You know what it takes to get through each day
So do what you have to to make it okay
And try not to worry about being strong
Just learn from the things that sometimes you do wrong
And keep looking up to the heavens above
Ask God to bless you with His loving touch
We live and we hope, we strive and we dream
Don't ever give up, and someday they'll be*

♡ *Poem 64*

Who Lord, But You

Who understands me but You Lord
You know why I cry when there's no reason to Lord
Who really loves me but You Lord
Through my failures, my mistakes, even the wrong I do Lord
Who really hears me but You Lord
You hear those unspoken words that say what I can't Lord
Who really cares but You Lord
You are always there when I lose my way Lord
Who will never forsake me Lord
Who won't lead me astray Lord
Who will always watch over me Lord
Who will hear when I pray Lord
Who Lord, but You

Babette Bailey

Poem 65 ♡

I Pray

You look at me with a wondering eye
I look at you and I wonder why
You're so young, so fake, or so it seems
But maybe you've lived more than I see
I wonder what goes on inside your mind
Feels like I've forgotten what being young was like
I hope, I pray for your sake and mine
You'll find the Lord and be saved in time
And we'll all live in a better place
Where no-one has to wear an unhappy face
If only I knew what was behind
The evil, the pain, all that's unkind
If only I knew when I was young too
But I didn't so I know that I can't fault you
So I pray

♡ *Poem 66*

Before

Before you look for my mistakes
Before you look down on me
Before you turn and walk away
Look at your own history

Before you say what's on your mind
Before you act like you're above me
Before you look so hard at my life
Look at yourself, what do you see

Are you all that you dreamed you'd be someday
Did you make mistakes along the way
Were there times when you went astray
Or didn't want to face another day
Have you ever stepped over the line
Well, before you judge me, or my kind
Before you take another step
Before you speak words that don't help
Remember to treat me as yourself
And consider if you should say anything else

Babette Bailey

Dark And Light

Could it be that everything has its dark and its light
Its good and bad, joy and sorrow, its lows and its highs
Love a very wonderful thing when its in the light of day
But when night comes many times, love seems to fade away
Children at times so very innocent and sweet
But when darkness comes around, they're like an unsolved mystery
In music there are some happy songs, some dancing songs, some love songs
But too there are some bad songs, some losing songs, and some sad songs
With friends there are those you know they're real and they're true
Then there are those who are only there to spitefully use and hurt you
The church, though it definitely has its light, its good and its right
Still has some areas where it's sometimes dark as night

♡ *Poem 68*

Immature

So young, is it over, I don't think so
Though at times you may feel it's not worth going on
Sometimes I feel that very same way
But we just have to take it day by day
Always thinking we wanna do right
Giving in to temptation, and losing the fight
I've learned the fight is in our minds
When we think we're defeated, we lose every time
If only our minds would fall in line
Cast out every thought of the negative kind
We could endure to the end, and we could win
No matter what battles we come up against
Have you ever wronged or hurt anyone
Did you stop to consider the damage you'd done
Imagine the pain you feel sometimes
It's probably just what they felt like
But though you're kind of immature now
In time you'll grow then wonder how
You used to be immature

Babette Bailey

Faces

You've worn so many faces
Played so many roles
Done so many tasks
Reached so many goals
Been so many things
In so many lives
Touched so many people
At so many times
You've always done
What you had to do
You've always hung in there
You've always come through
Now you've accomplished
Another task
And will soon wear
Yet another mask
No matter what face you wear
What holds true
Is the fighter, the winner
The champion in you

♡ *Poem* 70

Sisters

*So many things we've shared
As we've grown through the years
Reflecting on good and bad times
Our laughter and our tears
We've shared our fears and dreams
Our dresses and our shoes
We've shared our bows and make up
Our toys and secrets too
Although we had our fights
They were always soon forgotten
And the name-calling I know
Were a part of our growing lessons
Though time has separated us
It can never take away
The precious and special moments
That remain with us always
Those memories now they bring
Joy and laughter to our hearts
And reminds us sometimes love is distant
But it never falls apart*

Babette Bailey

Poem 71 ♡

Darling I Love You

I was thinking of you
What you always say
That I never take time
Out of my day
To just say my darling I love you

You say I never
Take the time to call
Or send you roses
Or go by the mall
To pick up something that might show you darling I love you

So today I'm taking
Not only a minute
But I'm putting some
Special effort in it
I realize how much darling I love you

I'm saying I'm sorry
For the times before
That I haven't made you
Feel adored
Believe me, darling I love you

I hope that now
Your beautiful smile
Will once again
Light up my life
I love you! I love you! I love you!

A Glimpse Into My Heart

♡ Poem 72

Love, Tell Me Where You Are

Love! Love! Love!
I've been sitting here thinking about love
Trying to find the meaning in my heart
I've been waiting for love, and hoping for love
Love tell me where you are?
Here I am
Where I can't see?
That's because you're thinking about you, not me
What, love, why can't you just make things plain?
OK, first stop searching for me with your brain
Search with your heart, now, what are you looking for?
For some romance, some flowers, and some gifts galore
See, your selfish, always thinking about yourself
Love is being considerate of someone else
Well, how can I love them, if I don't love me?
Of course love yourself, but your priorities
What you give, is what you receive
The seeds you sow, determine what you reap
So giving is receiving is what you're trying to say?
And love is first giving my own heart away?
That's right, just Jesus He gave His life
He loved us so, He was willing to die
Wow, that's deep; but that was Jesus Christ
That's right and He's The Way, The Truth and The Life
He set the example, He paved the way
He is True Love, He is the Agape
So seek His Way, His Truth and His Life
No matter what you're trying to find
And remember your seeds, giving is the key
Thanks love, I've got it now, sow love and love I'll reap
Then when love comes, it won't go
Simply because I don't know how to sow
I can see it now, love overflowing
I won't know whether love is coming or going
Love! Love! Love!

Babette Bailey

Additional Works
by Babette Bailey

Please be on the lookout for additional works:

Books of Poetry
Poetic Calendars
Greeting Cards
Home Décor / Canvas Prints
Other Writings &
Songs of Inspiration

Please like and follow me at **Babette's Creative Writing** Facebook page or contact me by email at babettebailey64@gmail.com. Let's partner for the Gospel's sake: conferences, special events, poetry readings, or study groups. Discounted bulk book orders are also available, please email me for more details.

If you would like a specific poem personalized for yourself or a gift, please contact me directly. Various sized prints are available for framing, along with, ready for display canvas home décor.

Sincerely,

Babette Bailey

www.ingramcontent.com/pod-product-compliance
Lightning Source LLC
Chambersburg PA
CBHW071507070526
44578CB00001B/465